Contents

What are harsh habitats? 4

Mighty mountains 6

Deep, dark sea 10

Steamy rainforests 14

Freezing cold Poles 16

Deadly deserts 20

Going underground 24

Concrete jungle 26

Quiz: What am I? 28

Glossary 30

Find out more 31

Index 32

What are harsh habitats?

Did you know that animals and plants live in some of the hottest, coldest, highest, and wettest places on Earth? The places where plants and animals live are called habitats.

EXTREME NATURE

HARSH HABITATS

Anita Ganeri

www.raintreepublishers.co.uk
Visit our website to find out
more information about
Raintree books.

To order:
☎ Phone 0845 6044371
🖹 Fax +44 (0) 1865 312263
🖳 Email myorders@raintreepublishers.co.uk

Customers from outside the UK please telephone +44 1865 312262

Raintree is an imprint of Capstone Global Library
Limited, a company incorporated in England and Wales
having its registered office at 7 Pilgrim Street, London,
EC4V 6LB – Registered company number: 6695582

Text © Capstone Global Library Limited 2013
First published in hardback in 2013
Paperback edition first published in 2014
The moral rights of the proprietor have
been asserted.

Edited by Dan Nunn, Rebecca Rissman,
  and Catherine Veitch
Designed by Cynthia Della-Rovere
Picture research by Tracy Cummins
Production by Alison Parsons
Originated by Capstone Global Library
Printed and bound in China by CTPS

ISBN 978 1 406 23789 4 (hardback)
16 15 14 13 12
10 9 8 7 6 5 4 3 2 1

ISBN 978 1 406 23794 8 (paperback)
17 16 15 14 13
10 9 8 7 6 5 4 3 2 1

British Library Cataloguing in Publication Data
Ganeri, Anita
Harsh habitats. -- (Extreme nature)
577.5'8-dc22
A full catalogue record for this book is available from
the British Library.

Acknowledgements
We would like to thank the following for permission to
reproduce photographs: Corbis p. 27 (© Michael Durham/
Visuals Unlimited); FLPA p. 21 (Konrad Wothe/Minden
Pictures); Getty Images pp. 7 (Arctic-Images), 10 (Karen
Gowlett-Holmes), 24 (Stephen Alvarez); istockphoto p. 14
(12924648); National Geographic Stock pp. 11, 12, 18
(NORBERT WU/MINDEN PICTURES); Photolibrary pp. 6
(Juan Carlos Munoz/age footstock), 9 (Superstock), 13
(Marevision Marevision), 19 (Steven Kazlowski), 26 (Crispin
Hughes); Shutterstock pp. 4 (© Petrova Maria), 5 (© Zacarias
Pereira da Mata), 8 (© 2009 fotofriends), 15 (© Dmitry
Savinov), 16 (© Witold Kaszkin), 17 (© Jan Martin Will),
20 (© Galyna Andrushko), 22 (© Patrick Poendl), 23
(© Alexander Yu. Zotov), 25 (© Ivan Kuzmin).

Cover photograph of Namib Desert reproduced with
permission of Shutterstock (© Pichugin Dmitry). Background
photograph of the cracked earth reproduced with permission
of Shutterstock (© vadim kozlovsky).

Every effort has been made to contact copyright holders
of material reproduced in this book. Any omissions will
be rectified in subsequent printings if notice is given to
the publisher.

Some words are shown in bold, **like this**. You can find
out what they mean by looking in the glossary.

DID YOU KNOW?
Plants and animals living in harsh habitats need special **features** to **survive**.

Mighty mountains

High up on a mountain, it is very cold with **gale-force** winds. The slopes may be bare and rocky, or they may be covered with ice and snow. So how do mountain plants and animals **survive**?

Vicuñas live in the Andes Mountains, in South America. They have thick coats to keep them warm.

Mountain goats are excellent climbers. Their **hooves** have sharp edges for gripping on to rocks. They also have pads that stop them from slipping.

Elfin trees grow very low to the ground.
This keeps them out of the wind.

Deep, dark sea

Deep down in the sea, it is pitch black and cold. Many deep-sea fish make their own lights. The lights are made of billions of tiny, glowing **bacteria**.

The anglerfish's light helps it to spot **prey**.

Flashlight fish have lights under their eyes. They can turn their lights off by covering them with skin. This helps them to escape from enemies.

light

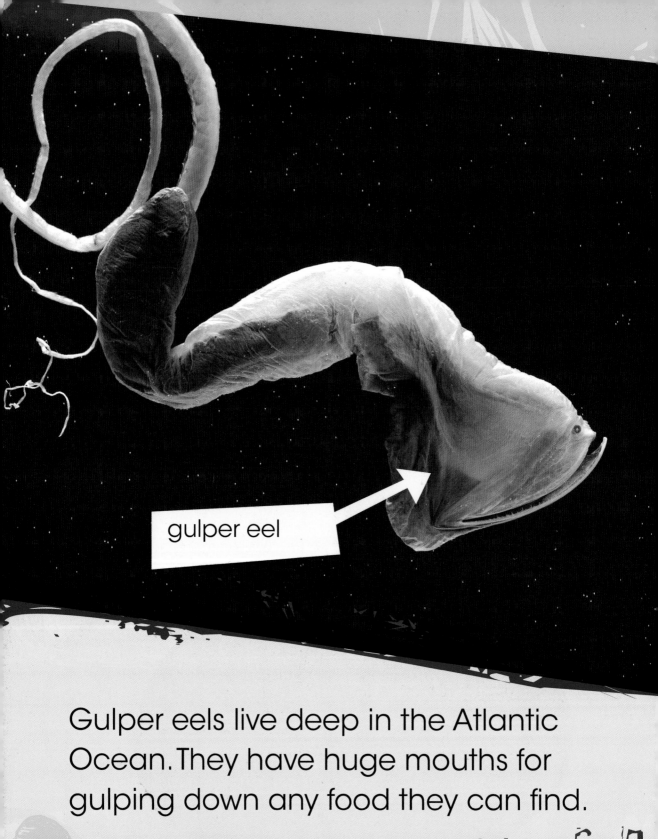

gulper eel

Gulper eels live deep in the Atlantic Ocean. They have huge mouths for gulping down any food they can find.

This snailfish is found deep in the ocean.

Steamy rainforests

Rainforests are hot and wet. They can be dangerous places to live in. Many animals have tricks for staying safe. Poison dart frogs have brightly coloured skin to warn hungry birds that they are deadly **poisonous**.

DID YOU KNOW?

Poison dart frogs get their name because people have used their poison to create poison darts.

Freezing cold Poles

The Arctic (North Pole) and Antarctica (South Pole) are the coldest and iciest places on the planet. In winter, the temperature in the Arctic can fall below -35°C!

Polar bears live in the Arctic. They have thick, oily fur with a thick layer of fat underneath. This keeps them warm and dry.

Ice fish

The seas around the North and South Poles are cold and icy. Ice fish in Antarctica have a special chemical in their blood that stops their bodies from freezing.

Weddell seals use their large teeth to gnaw, or chew, breathing holes in the ice.

Deadly deserts

Deserts can be baking hot in the daytime. Many desert animals spend the day in cool **burrows** underground.

DID YOU KNOW?
The temperature in the Sahara Desert can reach 45°C in the day.

Fennec foxes in the Sahara Desert in Africa have huge ears. Their ears give off heat, which helps the foxes to keep cool.

Deserts are very dry places. It is difficult for animals and plants to find water. Camels store water in their bodies. They can go for days without drinking.

DID YOU KNOW?
In parts of the Atacama Desert in Chile, it has not rained for hundreds of years.

Going underground

Caves are underground spaces. They form when rain and river water carve the rocks away. Caves are usually dark and damp.

DID YOU KNOW?

Some cave fish cannot see. They do not need to see in the dark caves.

Caves make good **roosting** places
for animals such as bats. Bats cling
upside down on the cave walls.

Concrete jungle

A busy, noisy city can be a harsh habitat. But many animals, such as foxes, **raccoons**, and **coyotes**, have moved into cities. This is because their wild homes are under threat.

raccoon

Animals find shelter in gardens and buildings. They find food in dustbins and rubbish tips.

Quiz: What am I?

Read the clues, then try to work out "What am I?". Find the answers at the bottom of page 29. But guess first!

1) I live on a mountain.
I have sharp **hooves**.
I am good at climbing.
What am I?

2) I have a big mouth.
I am a type of eel.
I live in the deep sea.
What am I?

3) I am **poisonous**.
I live in the **rainforest**.
I have brightly-coloured skin.
What am I?

4) I have thick, white fur.
I live in the Arctic.
I have thick fat under my skin.
What am I?

5) I am a type of fox.
I have big ears.
I live in the desert.
What am I?

Answers: **1)** mountain goat **2)** gulper eel **3)** poison dart frog
4) polar bear **5)** fennec fox.

29

Glossary

bacteria tiny living things

burrow hole that an animal digs in the ground

coyote dog-like animal that lives in
North America

feature special body part, pattern, or type
of behaviour

gale-force describes a very strong wind found
in a storm or high in the mountains

hooves hard coverings on a goat or horse's
feet

poisonous containing a substance that can
harm or kill

prey animal that is hunted for food

raccoon small furry animal from North America
that has a bushy striped tail

rainforest forest that is warm and wet all
year round

roost rest or sleep on a perch, such as a tree
branch or cave wall

survive stay alive

Find out more

Books

Habitat Explorer series, Greg Pyers (Raintree, 2006)

Horrible Habitats series, Sharon Katz Cooper (Raintree, 2010)

Survivors: Living in the World's Most Extreme Places, Ross Piper (A & C Black, 2010)

Websites

environment.nationalgeographic.com/ environment

This National Geographic website covers a range of habitats.

www.bbc.co.uk/nature/adaptations

This website contains lots of information about how animals survive in extreme habitats, with brilliant colour photographs.

Index

anglerfish 10
Antarctica 16, 18
Arctic 16, 17
Atacama Desert 23

bacteria 10
bats 25

camels 22
cave fish 24
caves 24–25
cities 26–27
coyotes 26

deserts 20–23

Elfin trees 9

fennec foxes 21
flashlight fish 11
foxes 21, 26

gulper eels 12

ice fish 18

mountain goats 8
mountains 6–9

North and South Poles
    16–19

oceans and seas
    10–13, 18

poison dart frogs
    14–15
polar bears 17

raccoons 26–27
rainforests 14–15

snailfish 13
Weddell seals 19